WORK LIFE

WORK LIFE
PAUL KANE

Turtle Point Press, New York

FOR MY TEACHERS   *But do your work, and I shall know you.*   EMERSON

CONTENTS

III. PSYCHE

IV. LIKE LIFE ITSELF

V. ARGUMENT FROM DESIGN

WORK LIFE

KNOWING

There came a day when to hear an airplane,
whether hard-edged drone or high whine,
gave one pause. We never were innocent,
only incurious within our managed lives,
worshipping household gods, lending unawares
our good name to a curse in others' mouths.
What has befallen us befell the world
a long time ago—long before we forgot
the club, the knife, the whip were ours too,
that the land absorbed blood as readily as rain.
Look at the garden and the order of these flowers:
circle within circle, like a dance or
a beautiful song that catches the breath.
It is mid-afternoon in late summer,
the sky's high dome of blue almost infinite.
Layers of sound separate out, each
a different register: the wind in the trees,
the cicadas in the grass, the birds calling
and twittering, and the wind chime ringing
pure notes, improvising a melody.
The eyes behold and are held by color—
the red barn, blue door, all the shades of green
and the riot of the garden. Even
the long shadows are clarifying.
Set this world on fire, you will know its worth.

1

I. A PORTENT

A PORTENT
FOR DNR

That cry in the woods, like none I ever heard,
sent up a racket of crows, a fury of wings
by the edge of the stream. That sound—as if

non-human anguish deeper than deep woods
lay at the heart of things—was fingernails
on chalkboard to the nerves, but a nervousness

every creature shared, bordering on fear.
I went into the woods and saw, without seeing—
feeling and hearing instead—a wind like wings,

a brown embodiment swift, and all but silent.
The next day it came again, announcing itself
amid its tumult on a high dead branch

overlooking us: a Great Horned Owl in daylight
shrieking that calamitous cry—and I cannot
bear to tell you the sorrows that followed.

5

TO MAKE A DESERT

They make a desert and call it peace.
      CALGACUS, on the Romans, AD 83

How will they remember us, the dead?
As a cause—a just cause—or simply an end?

And when we, like traces of shooting
stars, have visited our stripes upon the world

and in our turn are gone, how will we
be remembered by those who follow, those who

will have overcome us? The victors
who write also read the history of their

conquests. Will they read this: that we who
began with the word liberty in our mouths

ended with blood on our hands? That we
who surrendered freedom for security

lost both? That we fell into line with
history, and like others before turned brutal

with wealth and power and self-interest?
There are those alive now who will die of us,

each canceling out a sacrifice
by one who fought to save us from empires.

Who will save us from ourselves?

TWO TREES

I. WHAT WE HEAR

There is a tree falling in our back lot,
a willow, gigantic and scarred, with torn limbs
hanging at oblique angles, its base a tangle
of vines and wild rose. It is falling slowly,
imperceptibly, except for the daily
increase in its lean: gravity asserting
dominion over inertia—which is
to say, time has overtaken it.
As the tree falls, it makes no sound except
for the rasping of branches that graze one another
in the breezes. Each storm that blows hard foretells
demise, but this morning, despite the gale
winds of last night and the lashing rain, there
it is, at odds with the rest of the angular woods:
obdurate, proud, inexorable, old—
older by a day. When it falls at last,
completing the half-arc of its life, we will
hear it in the hollows of the heart.

II. WHAT COMES AFTER

Years ago another tree, a willow larger than the one in the
    far field,
fell in a whirlwind on a hot summer night. Its crash brought
    us out
into the wild air, and where the tree had been was a darkness
we had never seen before, a gap through which no star shone,
no planet revolved. We were struck and ached with the loss.
In the morning, the tree lay like a fallen giant, broken
though propped on limbs like elbows, its crown crushed
and half-buried in the marshy ground. It seemed the wreckage
of a hope that had towered before us, defining the space of our
movements and dwelling. All that would change now, we knew,
and were bitter because we never looked for the alteration.
Who can anticipate change? And yet we know nothing stays
    the same
but change. Where crows had once alighted in the upper boughs,
deer now came at daybreak to strip the succulent branches,
    a windfall
that must have startled them on their circuit through our
    domain.
For sure, we thought the tree dead and let it lie where it fell.
But now another tree grows out of it, for some lateral root
    remained

buried and nourished the trunk. Other suckers have appeared too,
yet the main life runs in the sap of the vertical branch, which
    already wears
a green crown of its own. It will outlive us, taking on its final
    form—
and that is a hope, as death makes way for what comes after.

ADMIRALTY BAY
BEQUIA. THE GRENADINES

The man on the mast swings in his red cloth chair,
working to fix a snag in the mainsail rigging:
the labor of others is more compelling
than our own. The man in the chair raises and lowers
himself as a water taxi skims past in bright
Caribbean colors, with "African Pride" painted
below the gunwales, red on a yellow background,
like a national flag of dispossession.
Despair is the fruit of disparity, and where
it ripens it never falls far from the free.
The sailboat will cruise away leaving money
in its wake. The motorboat circles the harbor,
catching fares and chasing fairness in the guise
of freedom. No nation is an island, says
Geo-Politics; no island is a nation,
says Multinational Markets. To develop
importance, you import development
but you outsource sovereignty.
                              The man in the chair
knows the precariousness of in between
but his yacht attests to wealth that's grounded in
securities. "African Pride" cuts his engine
and glides to the dock, smooth and practiced,
professional. The yachties are set to sail:

the auxiliary engines billow diesel
fumes on the water as the boat finds a way through
the harbor out of the bay to the open sea.
Naked children, blond and bronzed, with orange floats
on their arms, splash among the waves on the beach.

A MYTH OF JUSTICE

When he died his sense of justice was revealed,
distributive and proportional, not

the mere equation one divided by two
(though two came to be divided by one

in the end), but each according to need,
as the ancient Greeks divined in Athens.

To the daughter who had the least but gave
the most—and of herself, for him—he left

more than to the wealthy son, so richly
deserving this lesson in equality.

But the brother had a different idea
of justice, and though the father was a man

with an iron will, the son sought to break
the Will, splitting the property evenly

for the sake of fairness and propriety.
The daughter, loathe to appear grasping,

concurred in her loss of independence.
And so it transpired, rich took from poor,

as if Politics rules even in death.
Justice, from her column in the courthouse,

winked at the brother and readjusted
the calibrations of her butcher's scale—

winked again, and slipped her blindfold back on.
In the mural on the wall of the rotunda,

Athena had narrowed her gray-green eyes,
the Furies gathering behind her.

NO PHOTO. GO HOME.

10.17.01

Upwind the air is rancid—
closer in, the eyes wince.

"No Photo. Go Home." says
the blue sheet on the brownstone.

At the barricades the wind
tears at faces of the missing.

Around us people mill
confounded by what remains.

Ground down to zero,
blackened, we smolder.

One more gust and it all breaks
into flame. No Photo. Go Home.

THE KOAN

I am the mask I wear and know as little
about the wearer as the puppet the puppeteer.

The life I live isn't mine, it lives through me
and I through it dance and strut on my strings

in counterfeit. If you told me about myself
I would not believe you, for how can I be other

than what I have known? When I die, who I am
will step out into the light to try another life,

while I—having passed away—will know all
and nothing. In the dark, I am riddled by doubt.

II. THIRD PARENT

THIRD PARENT

I.M. CHRISTINE NICHOLSON

I

Now that I have but one I think of you
as the third—neither substitute nor supplement
but a fact of nature, human nature, mine
and yours, as if it was always meant to be
incalculable, this new planet come
from another system into ours:
suddenly it was there and we never
questioned it or showed our astonishment.

"Don't *even* think of it," you would say
in that southern accent that never gave in
to English propriety or Australian drawl,
just as you never compromised where
everyone around you accommodated
the world: in little things—the things that matter.
It only ever took a whiff of attitude
for adoring friends to be shown the door.

Our love was a conspiracy, a pact
against the shoddy self that threatened
to undermine that wall of honesty
fronting your house, your heart's home.
On the one side, no; on the other, all the yes

19

the world could muster as a force,
for you lived *plein air*, spirited and open
to the light that shone around you and within.

II

One day you decided to be old.
Sitting in your armchair, reading
the daily paper, you must have told
yourself, "That's it, I won't be needing
appearances anymore," and went on to unfold
The Age, as if time in succeeding
intervals was nothing but a threshold
to the will, a way of proceeding
from day to day, in control.

But you were never old, you were young, always,
the way each morning is newer than the night
before, the way a memory dawns that has hung
a long time at the edge of the mind: the finite
return of an infinite series, a chorus sung
at the end of every verse to invite
the next and then the next, until the far-flung
song comes round again and we delight
to recognize the place where we'd begun.

You were that place for us, 40-O
we called it, an address only you could occupy,

though it never belonged to you, and so,
when you left, it ceased to exist, which is why
you never spoke of going back: my shadow,
you seemed to say, is always behind my
back when I face the sun. What do I owe
the past except to settle the accounts
I bring into the present as my special sorrow?

III

We have nowhere to go now, with every reason
to go: friends, professions, a group, and love
of the land and the light—all the circumference
of a life without the center, as if a void
were proof positive for the existence of God.

But we'll go back, and back, until we find
in the genealogy of the past the source
of a hope born of despair, some hill or field
to call our own, to call *to* our own: come
and walk with us over the common ground.

There is a long way to travel still, and our days
are numbered to the power of one.
All your days, on that single vigilant night,
were multiplied by zero, yielding infinity.
When the sun rose, you were everywhere.

21

AT OLANA
FOR SOPHIE & STEPHEN

On a blanket, spread out in the shade of an oak tree,
    cheese, bread, fruit and wine beside a garden
and a wall, the man's house behind, the scene he
    painted before us, river, mountains, sky
and above all light: we drank to you—the chilled
    Portuguese wine like bottled memory,
each sip a tang. And we spoke not of then but
    of now and next, and all that we could share
of happiness was there, even if we
    could not share it with you, neither now nor
later. But why do I tell you this? Is it
    because I no longer believe in later—that
it's all happening now and there is nothing
    I can do to stop it or slow it to a pace
I can walk to?
                    Let us dance a measure
    instead—to make free—and take up
this sorrow, turning it round and around until
    it is something else, something like praise of life
and the living and the dead, and say for now,
    just for this moment, that love is praise enough
and that the beauty laid out before us
    like a painting is another memory of you,
another taste of this Portuguese wine.

22

WIDOWER

There on the stoop alone
when all along we thought
he'd be the first to go.

So much said in that wave:
the hand languid—as though
moving through water.

I nod and walk by—words
are clumsier than gesture.
The body knows its own.

FOR MY FATHER DYING

I did my weeping a long time ago.
It was in Venice, on a family trip—
Planned for the fiftieth anniversary—
And I accompanied you back to the hotel
By vaporetto while the others went
On to see the horses of San Marco.

Golden June, Venice at its best, and you
Proposed martinis—a drink I never drink—
But down we went to the waterside bar
And despite our doubts the Italian bartender
Made good ones—knowing his Americans—
And it was a joy to be with you in enjoyment,

The youthful glint and manner back again
After so many years, and when I led
You to your room, then found my own, I lay
Down and the tears came. I wept long and hard
And knew it was for the day that comes
Sooner than tears anticipate.

THE NIGHT HERON

What are we to ask of a shadow?
At noon, night flickers around us
as we walk in the cold sun's light.

North by northeast, the wind changes.
We watch for the great blue heron,
wintering over, to return to the marsh.

We are smaller than the shadows
cast before us: greatcoats we cannot
put off, like time and the age.

Moonrise and nightfall. Pity, we say,
that the blue heron should be lost,
or absented from our sky.

DEAR MARGIE

I don't know what life looks like from the other
side of life, but I know what death looks like

from here: like sorrow and grief and loss
and people gathered in a long remembrance—

like a winter's shadow in the afternoon.
Dear Margie, do you smile on us because

we love you or because we don't understand?
When you died you left us your life—

you've finished with it, but we haven't,
and won't, until we've finished with our own.

Your life—that shining thing in your eyes,
that laugh, ebullient like a spring

in a mountain pool, and as generous in its flow.
Your life remains with us—

you don't need it now, but we do.
It was always part of ours anyway.

ENGRAVED

after The Other Vietnam Memorial

by CHRIS BURDEN

> Vertical rolodex, the copper sheets
> on panels hinged to a central pole
> swing freely with barely a sound.
> As if blind, I decipher the letters
> by touch, but white cotton gloves
> keep human oils at a distance
> from the three million names.

A MURDER OF CROWS

I.M. FRED GOODALL

Such a warm day for November—nature
preternatural—two cabbage moths
rise above the garden (where only orange
calendula still bloom), spiraling up
a white double helix high in the air, when
one suddenly drops, the other fluttering off—
lost now in shadows among the pine trees,
its companion invisible in the long grass.

Our world acts as a membrane directing the flow
of time in its singular forward direction,
but now and then something seeps through in reverse,
a backwash from the other side, like a check
valve that fails in the plumbing, or—if it serves
some purpose after all, beyond us—then
like a vitreous fluid weeping unnoticed through
the trabecular meshwork of the eye.

Driving across the black dirt fields a week
later, I recall what you said about
the gathering of crows at Pine Island
this one week of the year, for here they are
by the hundreds, gleaning perhaps, but most
simply still, as if waiting to pass through
to a negative world where they, in turn,
are white, their fluttering rippling time.

III. PSYCHE

PSYCHE

This mid-May morning, cool, cloudy and green
deepens the woods beyond, transforming the scene
into a world winter had nearly forgot
in the rigidity of angular thought.
It has been seven weeks now since that day
in Chicago, when the weather turned away
from winter and embraced all at once the spring.
It was my birthday, and the year's rebirth: starting
again—that time when the wind goes around you
gently rather than slicing straight through.
I walked to the Art Institute to buy
a book, *Uncontrollable Beauty*, that I
had seen the day before but wanted now.
It was warm and sunny enough to allow
for a turn in the sculpture garden outside,
so I went and, finding a bench unoccupied,
spent the next half hour in a repose of thought
turned toward the year past and what it had taught
me about living—and death—and trying
to wake up in a world so stupefying
that I despaired of anything more than
momentary wonderment, when what began
each time as a coming home to oneself
ended in alienation, all the wealth
of the gain wiped out in profit-taking,

selfhood slavishly aggrandizing
to itself what it never could earn: grace
born of the effortless effort to efface
identity for the sake of existing
right now, here, on this bench, first day of spring.

Writing in a little moleskin journal
I note, "The bells just rang in a cathedral
nearby, 10:45" and "I aspire
to my age," and then as if the Muses require
a truth: "to tell a falsehood you need first
to be false to yourself"—which is no worse
than most epigrammatic platitudes
by those who climb in the upper attitudes.
But the next entry begins the story:
"A butterfly just flew over and kissed me
on the head." I wouldn't write it that way now
(it sounds so twee), but that's exactly how
it struck me, except I was guessing it was
a butterfly—but then I knew, because
it flew into view a few feet away.
I marveled that it appeared on a day
so early in the year, with no other
warm days to herald it. In another
moment it was gone, as if ephemeral,
something metaphoric, not literal,
as when in *The Golden Ass* Apuleius
tells the story of the metamorphosis

of Psyche from mortal into goddess
beloved of Cupid, and thereafter Morris,
Pater and Bridges tell it again sculpted
in verse and prose the way Canova did
in marble or Burne-Jones and others in oils.
Psyche, ransacked for imagery like the spoils
of war, who began Keats's great run of odes,
fleshed out in allegories with lodes
of tantalizing meanings, as Love pursues
the Soul, but the Soul tested by what ensues
from treachery and disobedience
becomes immortal only through the guidance
of intercessors and its own burning want.
But the reader's desire isn't for a font
of allegorical wisdom, it's for
fulfillment, and the desire for more
diversion drives the narrative forward
through indirection or——to use the word
Aristotle deploys——the knot, the complex
knitting together of strands until what's next
is the unraveling into determinate
meaning——or so it seems for a minute
afterwards, before indeterminacy
of implication takes over and fancy
begins to play with the materials: 33
then a new version gets born that feels
truer to one's time and experience.
Take Psyche's father the King, for instance,

how he agrees, in despair, to sacrifice
his daughter for his kingdom—and though the price
is steep, so is the precipice disaster
has prepared for his ill-starred child to master
and he to draw back from. Granted his subjects
want no part of her doom, but still one objects
to the alacrity with which the ancients
offered up their own children. Such abhorrence
extends to Medea and Agamemnon—
poor Iphigenia! (unless you're conned
by Euripides' Hollywood mocking of
the story with his *deus ex machina*
in *Iphigenia in Tauris*)—but think
too of Isaac, with Abraham at the brink
of pious murder, willing to cut his son's
throat for God, whose own Son's crucifixion
becomes the type of them all. What is it
to sacrifice what Nature all but commits
us to sacrifice ourselves for—our issue?
Is it the unnatural we most value?
These myths cannot be said to mean anything,
they mean so much—too much for us to bring
them into the circuit of understanding.
They break out at anomalous points, expanding

in significance in ways that undermine
the apparent shape of the story. We find
ourselves ignoring details to spare
our readings—"There is no love," we say, "where

there is not trust," citing Cupid's abrupt flight
when burned by Psyche's treacherous lamplight.
But what god would trust a human? Cupid
may be smitten, but he isn't stupid.
These myths are portentous, meaning hovers
about them, visiting us like those lovers
at night conjoined swiftly and unbidden.

It was like that for me when, again, hidden
from view the butterfly returned and this time
stayed on the back of my head, as if a sign
from Heaven or Nature that I was blessed
or resembled a flower. We both were at rest
on that stone bench off the gravel path and I
had become ornamental while the butterfly
turned us symbiotic and sympathetic.
I was touched—delighted—by this poetic
circumstance, and thankful too that I had read
J. Allen Boone's *Kinship with All Life*, which led
me to think I might communicate—
rather than simply commune and wait
for my visitor to leave—since both of us
vibrate at the rate of life, homologous
too in the evolutionary sense
(if not homomorphic in size), and hence

expressive of a shared ground of being
and capable of embodying meaning.
And so I spoke to the insect out loud

(we were alone), saying how pleased and proud
I was that it had come, praising it as well
for its beauty and grace beyond parallel,
and all the while not feeling ridiculous
but happy to overcome self-consciousness
enough to be absurd and genuine,
to sit there and for those moments feel at one
with this tiny thing. Were I a Buddhist
this would be no great shakes, and for a nudist,
I suppose, such things happen all the time,
living so close to Nature as to have climbed
into her lap. But for me just to bare
my soul was enough——if soul were there——
and if enlightenment is the absolute
horizon, then I was as resolute
a seeker of truth for those minutes as
any robed in the Buddha's sermon of ash
and fire. What is freedom if not release
from identification with your beliefs?
When Emerson writes in "Circles" (as he's sure
to in any case), "I am God in nature;
I am a weed by the wall," the vast ebb
and flow are not of equal value——the web
of moods that entangles us defeats our will

(and to harness power is beyond our skill).
And yet the god of these rocks is a chaos
to the person when unleashed, and the cost
is loss of certainty that we know best

our own interests, as in fact the very worst
that can befall us is to gain what we most
desire—because we desire in the first place.
Subtle the snake, and we so eager to taste
forbidden fruit, the deception is all ours.

A moment's grace can come to us at all hours
and in any place, lighting up our world
or shattering it, with the pieces hurled
into that abyss of remorse, self-knowledge.
That's why we cling to beliefs as to a ledge,
believing that if we fall it's to our death—
which is true enough, for to draw our last breath
in this metamorphic sense is to enter
another stage, like the caterpillar
dissolving in the cocoon, from a larva
to a liquid protoplasmic pupa
which is the chrysalis—but really it's
a mystery, and solving its explicit
riddle is reserved for lepidopterists
such as Nabokov whose specialty consists
of appreciation for the "spiraling
unfolding of things in time," the startling
way that metaphors can metamorphize
into facts—the obverse of Thoreau's surmise
that facts are likely to flower into truths.
No wonder *Walden* was aimed at youths
puzzled by vocation, since a college

education is a cocoon of cordage
spun by the student munching on the leaves
of books—though in this case the butterfly weaves
and the caterpillar emerges instead.
This comes of teaching the branches of knowledge
but none of the roots, says Thoreau, so back
we go into the chrysalis to enact
again the process of decrystallizing
our beliefs, becoming human by dying
to that death-in-life Wordsworth called "a sleep
and a forgetting."
                    What memory does
the butterfly have of its previous
existence? The Venerable Bede
compares our life to the flight of a bird
through a banquet hall on a winter's night
while outside a storm rages—that respite
for the sparrow is all we know of living,
of the taking of life and of the giving:
out of the dark into the warmth and comfort
of the hall, and then again out—how short
a distance from end to end!—and of the rest
we know nothing, though the nothing we attest
to is not the same, for Bede, as *Nothingness*.

Is it a consoling image? At best
it suggests a cool reception beyond,
but then the eighth century would not respond
well to a doctrine unheroic and soft.

Later, the banqueting is sent aloft
into heaven and the storm moves inside.
And if, as Matthew wrote, no sparrow has died
apart from the Father, what of the birth
of the butterfly? No theologian worth
a pinch of salt would deny equal status,
but if Death is the *persona non gratis*
what do we do with Birth? Our first response
is joy, purest of emotions, and the wants
of the child elicit giving without
any regard for recompense—but note
the ambiguity the myths embody,
the Parcae, goddesses of destiny,
sometimes seated on celestial thrones
and other times represented as crones
ministering to the King of Hell.
In for a penny, in for a pound as well,
so why not talk to a butterfly?

Unlike Cupid, whose *modus operandi*
in his palace at night, bedding down Psyche,
was insistence upon anonymity,
I wanted visibility, so I asked
my visitor, as in a Renaissance masque,
to come forward like the deity she was
and reveal herself, if only because
I wished to acknowledge my benefactress
and extend our acquaintance. And so my guest,

in a visitation more than a visit,
fluttered down and landed on my hand. Is it
to be wondered at, the swelling of the heart?
A threshold was crossed and we were now part
of a larger whole that bound us together
and in doing so freed us up, whether
to be one, or two-in-one, or one-in-two,
it didn't matter, for what mattered to
us, in this advent, in this adventure,
was the joining, two creatures in nature
gone beyond what would be thought natural
into something so natural it was awful
to behold—to be held by this feeling
deepening into emotion, sealing
the bond between us as a shared consciousness,
or perhaps a consciousness sharing us.
Here was a doubleness, a mirroring effect
in which the other was oneself reflected
back, and since each was a mirror in turn
we resembled a cheval glass, which, we learn
in France, is called a "psyche," a large double
glass hinged on a rotating stand—a useful
image since the event could be deemed "psychic."
But even if we hold ourselves agnostic
on such matters, the experience speaks
for itself—in itself, of itself—for weeks,
in fact, it spoke to me and is speaking still.

But what of the butterfly? Up until
now I've said nothing of its appearance—
other than its appearance, its entrance
on the scene. My notebook (of which more later)
records the following to indicate her
size: medium. Precise, no? But then goes on:
"with brown and gold markings like a ribbon
on her wings, a fuzzy body, two lovely
antennae with gold tips." Subsequently,
I discovered she was a Banded Elfin,
which accounts for her early arrival, given
the time of year: these elves are among the first
to venture forth in the spring in a sunburst
of color, and with such a sweet dalliance
celebrate their renaissance in alliance
with the equinox—our annual re-birth
in this part of the hemispheric earth.
How strange, to think that as a child I chased
these insects across the fields and raced
about with the same instinct as my cats
today: if it moves away then pounce and kill.
I recall summer days in Cobleskill
when I would run with a fishing net
after monarchs and cabbage moths and yet
never know what to do with them when caught:
they were not lovely when dead, just an insect,
slightly noisome and even pitiful.
It was the same with grasshoppers on High School

Hill above our house, in the layered outcrop
of rock where they sunned themselves and hopped
about or flew suddenly with a whirr
away from my outstretched hands, a blur
of motion, a frightful fear in flight.
If I trapped them, they spat as if to fight
to the end, but in the end I let them go,
as it was only the chase that mattered.
And though scores of them each summer get splattered
on my windshield, I loathe harming insects.
The impulse to kill may be a reflex
from evolution but it's a question
then of how far we've evolved if when
faced with something beautiful and graceful
our first response is to pull out a pistol.
Still, I'm alarmed when a drowsy wasp
drops on my hand—an adrenaline gasp
too fast for any fine opinion
I may have about treating the dominion
of insects as an egalitarian—
and since I'm not a vegan vegetarian,
I should back off a bit and admit
that even a butterfly as exquisite
as my Elfin might ordinarily
elicit a fidgeting—only rarely
am I possessed enough to be possessed
by a spirit as charming as Psyche, dressed
up in entomological finery.

So it was—if you will—a mystery
to me how everything came together
that morning in Chicago when the weather
brought us both out to enjoy and join
each other. And, as if nature were toying
with us in a mutual observation,
the Elfin began an investigation
of my left hand with her proboscis—
a more delicate organ of gnosis
I could not imagine: a black thread
come alive and yet connected to the head
as a feeding tube for sucking nectar,
not to mention serving as inspector.
An elephant's trunk is much the same,
and as *proboscis* is the formal name
for our snout, the phrase "nosing around" makes sense,
or in this case sense makes knowledge, hence
the Elfin's exploration of the index
finger of my right hand, which in all respects
resembled a caress as much as a deft
reconnaissance. So, as she sat now on my left
thumb, so lightly I could hardly feel her,
and probed under my nail with her feeler,
she seemed to me immeasurably kind,
tracing my cuticle as if to find
there the secret of my being, where flesh
meets carapace, soft the hard.

I wished

43

her well and resumed my little patter
about how beautiful she was, and rather
pleased with my praise it seemed, she turned around
and walked up and down my hand and then found
her way on to the bright surface of my book,
and there opened and closed her wings, and took
the sunlight and cast a shadow of herself
upon the blank page—as if to say, the wealth
of expectation invested here
is an image of the heart, an austere
hope visible in outline but awaiting
words that go beyond adumbrating
the form to introducing us to the life:
words beyond words, and care beyond strife.

When I told this story to our friend Erik,
who shares an interest in the esoteric,
along with Michael and Ritambhara—
sitting out on the back veranda
having breakfast (hominy and Taylor's ham),
mid-morning, May ninth—we were a pentagram
of people (counting Tina) and the magic
figure we composed lent a certain logic
to the conversational flow that carried
us along—or aloft—however varied
the topic, until depositing us here
at this point in my tale. It was crystal clear
to Erik that what occurred was precisely

what Augustine would have described (concisely,
and in prose) as an illustration in God's
Book of Nature: for when the butterfly treads
my unwritten page opening her wings
and shutting them, she extends the blessings
of the Spirit—coterminous with the Word—
upon us both, her wings resembling
pages fluttering in the wind and trembling
with the animating force of the Divine.
What impassioned exhortations would the Good
Saint not have made if this experience should
have happened to him? What pluperfect
subjunctives would he not have employed to perfect
his Latin eloquence? Alas, that it fell
to me to narrate this event, and to tell
it in rhyming couplets and stumbling feet.
As Michael said that morning, the complete
story, with all its embellishments, isn't
as interesting finally as the hint
the tale gives of how Nature opens to us
if only we open to it, just
as Truth is revealed to us in Justice.
The fact that my Elfin accomplice
was the occasion for the occasion
simply underscores the conscious phase in   45
which I found myself: open, yes, but
also at work upon him who would shut
the doors of perception: me, who stands

in the way when standing aside demands
an effacement before the other I am.
My Psyche came to me the way an iamb
comes to a poet: first, sit down to write. "Do
your work," says Emerson, "and I shall know you."

The butterfly confirmed what I already
knew: that Psyche, she ain't no lady—
Cupid took her; she married him on the spot.
A bow-and-arrow marriage, call it, but not
because either was unwilling. He left her
in the dark (as he came to her, in a purr
of passion) regarding his identity,
but she, betrothed to a beast, an entity
meant to devour her, made the beast
with two backs in coupling with Cupid—at least,
we could say, she took pleasure where she found it.
O lovely Psyche, ravishing spirit,
you turn the heads of gods! Even Venus
you won over (and to have kept Jove's penis
out of the story—that's an accomplishment!).
So, confronting someone with a penchant
like Psyche's, we must beware of thinking
her innocent or shy, demure, a shrinking
violet afraid of Apollo. Remember,
she too became a goddess, full-fledged member
of Club Med at Mount Olympus, and this
astonishing metamorphosis

suggests untold power, since no story
comes down about her later exploits, or we
would know more concerning the transformation
from human to divine—not to mention
how it is that everyone now is said
to possess a psyche. Mind or Soul, the head
is at the top of our list of puzzlements
while all the while the heart supplements
what it means to be mortal. The heartless
gods aren't to be toyed with, but kept apart, lest
they kill us with premature self-knowledge.
Better the dawn come slowly: the water's edge
is the liminal point where we can survive
and still behold vastness. In the dark night, dive
into that phosphorus sea and you may be found
washed up on the shore at daybreak, the ground
of your being no longer something you can stand.
So it was a blessing that from elfland
my Psyche came unbidden and kindly,
revealing a knowledge I had blindly
concealed from myself, that the visible
world is invisible until we're able
to recognize how interconnected
we are as expressions of life—directed
by what is greater than our will, the gods
of the moment when time stands still. The odds
are, that all our learning is recovery
of what we once knew, and the discovery

that the heart remembers is the beginning
which is also an end: the winnowing
of the chaff that leaves hard kernels—wisdom—
as seeds to grind, prepare and eat for freedom.

For five minutes the butterfly stayed with me—
much as she remains now—and what she
did next I thought very witty. Across
the path, ten yards away, like a long-lost
creature out of time past, a red sculpture
by Calder, in bolted steel—a rupture
of the air in flowing form: it was called
The Dragon, though its overall shape, installed
there in the garden, suggested more
a giant butterfly poised to soar
on uplifted wings. Off went my Elfin,
darting towards the dragon and, with a spin,
she looped around it once, wings to wings,
as if to say, all these man-made things
are part of my world too—let us share them
with a joy of belonging. What emblem
could have been more fitting? She disappeared
then, among the trees, and I had a weird
sense of having been given a gift

on my birthday, something to uplift
me for the coming year, drawing me out
of present sorrows where pain and doubt
had reigned as the past sad year's legacy

of loss, until this spring day when my Psyche
emerged in a rebirth from what seemed
a death but was only a stage, a dream
from which she awoke and waking me—
in turn—made of us both a mythology.
My last notebook entry, where she came to rest,
reads simply: "I have never felt so blessed."

IV. LIKE LIFE ITSELF

LIKE LIFE ITSELF

Nulla riposa della vita come
la vita. UMBERTO SABA

From a table on the terrace the square
opens out in successive waves of attention.
The woman sits before a glass of wine—
her talisman or offering
to the genius of the place.
                              She is not young,
but neither is she old enough to know
how rare these moments can become in time.
But for now, the scene in a wash of light
is more vivid than perception accounts for:
the flower cart with cascades of nosegays,
unhurried couples strolling or sitting near
the little brimming fountain of worn marble,
the pastel buildings wearing balconies,
all are like an unfolding revelation
in the heart.
                              At her ease, nothing could be
easier than this fall into being
or beauty or just life itself—from which there is
no rest but for moments like these in the square.   53

DOO TOWN
FOR PETER PORTER

Just off the A9, en route to Port Arthur,
Here close by the Blowhole,
Tasman's Arch and the Devil's Kitchen,
the little settlement of Doo
revels in its punning nomenclature.
The vying houses try to out-do one
another: Doo Drop In, Nothing to Doo,
Diggery Doo, Morning Doo—
we are the punning species,
looking for ways to escape
enclosures of language,
the incarcerations of identity:
give us a gap in common sense
and we're quick to brave chained
dogs of earnest and deadly probity.
At Port Arthur, only eleven
men ever escaped, though one at least
perished in the Bush, the leg irons
still fixed to his skeleton.
They were poets every one.
Guarded by the criminally sane,
we go about our business in the modern
panopticon, while miles of videotape
record inanities in the bank,

the supermarket, outside the apartments
of the wealthy, before the consulates
of the civilized nation-states.
In the unconsecrated church at
Port Arthur—built by those hardened
boy criminals from Point Puer,
who cut the stone, fashioned
the bricks and carved the woodwork—
we stand in the open space (the roof
burnt down from a trash fire
next door) thinking, what
at this point, in this anomalous
place, can one do? Our escapes—
our escapades—may be momentary
freedoms, but this spot seethes
with unlawful provocation.
It is no nightmare from which
we simply awake—and for those in
hammocks slung low across the cells
the morning sun was the eye
of despair. Do unto others, the
golden rule of Tasmania. One could
do worse than live in the village of Doo.

TEEN TOWN
FOR THE CLASS OF '68

Off North Grand and beside the creek
on a dead-end road lies Teen Town.
We hung out there, biding our time
as the '60s rolled in on the air waves:
Beach Boys, Beatles and Byrds beat
in our blood like mainlined hormones
till we got every song by heart.
The girls gossiped and we played hoops.

Holmes flicks a pass behind his back
to Helme, who hits a fade-away jump;
the Pendergast twins clear the boards;
and Broph gives an elbow and a bump.

When a .45 was a record
not a gun—that was a .22—
a .33 was cool, but radio
ruled in a GTO with 4
on the floor and a 389.
At 16 we drove and 18 was legal
but drinking was a Teen Town taboo,
when girls gossiped and we played hoops.

Sylvia, Sue, Lonnie and Barb
had the right look, wore the right garb.
Songs the end-all, dance the be-all,
Teen Town revolved around b-ball.

We looked for action on Saturday
night, with a fistfight as good as
a movie: we knew our roles and
played our parts with a courage born
from fear of failing—that rush
of adrenaline was counterfeit
hate, and friendship the real emotion,
while girls gossiped and we played hoops.

Holmes flicks a pass behind his back
to Helme, who hits a fade-away jump;
the Pendergast twins clear the boards;
and Broph gives an elbow and a bump.

On a rainy day we'd go inside
and try to tease the girls, but girls
know more and decide who's in—
and if you're out you never know why—
so we'd do the dance of not wanting
to dance the Twist, Swim, Pony and Jerk,
Mashed Potato and Locomotion.
Then the girls gossiped and we played hoops.

Sylvia, Sue, Lonnie and Barb
had the right look, wore the right garb.
Songs the end-all, dance the be-all,
Teen Town revolved around b-ball.

Off North Grand and beside the creek
on a dead-end road lies Teen Town.
The decades pass but the rites are the same,
the only change is in the pronoun.

A WHITER SHADE OF PALE

"… although my eyes were open"

In '68 I sported a Panic Button on my blazer—
pushed, it read "Things will get worse before
they get worse." After the assassinations, I threw
it away. On edge, we were now living on the edge.
Across the hall, Drexler, the quiet kid from Belgium,
played Procol Harum full blast whenever
he left the room, the door wide open.
Conformity consisted of learning "how to think
for ourselves," but we knew one another by our
oddities, while the teachers knew us for our failings.
That year, falling in love sent me stumbling backwards—
the real fall came later, when Signe took up with Ramseur,
the handsome hockey star who insisted we arm wrestle
because I could hit a ball farther than he.
My roommate, Leep, the math genius from Menlo Park,
was California cool; Arader, a Main Line Mensa
miles gloriosus; but Schiffer was pure New York.
I tried making a virtue of my virtues
but when I puzzled things out, the pieces never fit.
Prep school prepared you to succeed, but no one
prepared us for success—that was a blank
we would have to fill on our own, or not,
like Drexler's empty room blaring "A Whiter Shade of Pale."

Not long ago, I heard that song again by chance
on the radio, and these memories welled up
quick—a pool in a clearing, spring-fed
and coruscating. Those pieces of the past
coalesced suddenly into a whole—
beyond the pain of nostalgia or wistfulness
for lost youth: a presence, instead, an intensity
so tensile the insight stretches out past
the instant of its moment—as when you
are perfectly happy or in complete despair.
And in the midst of it, I thought of Drexler
and wondered about that song haunting the radio,
about why he did what he did and why it affected
me so much then and now decades after.
"Whatever happened to Drexler?" we ask, as if
we could say what it was that had happened to us
from a point of view outside ourselves.
Two days later—no, thirty-six years later—I got
an email from Drexler reading, "Remember me?"

TWO-LINERS

MY FATHER'S NEUROPATHY

I've staggered out of a lot of bars, he says,
but never into one before.

POETIC LICENSE

"Live Free or Die!" cries New Hampshire;
"First in Flight," North Carolina demurs.

SIGN ON AN UPSTATE JAIL IN WINTER

Any prisoner not back by six o'clock
will be locked out.

SIGN ON AN UPSTATE FARM

Anyone found here at night
will be found here in the morning.

NATIONAL PASTIME

Football will supplant baseball when we
start wearing helmets on the street.

CLICHÉD

Give him enough rope
and he'll hang you.

AT THE POE MUSEUM

RICHMOND, VIRGINIA

In the lurid red room a DVD
Of "The Raven" plays, interpreted as Poe
Himself performed it with a heebie jeebie
Elocution fueled by the libido
Swooning women exuded in rococo
Hats. In a corner, a bust of Pallas
Regards the busts of Doré nudes in the throes
Of "most stormy" passions, fed by a malice
In that "Nevermore!" croaked by the accomplice.
Nevermore? Rather, More! More!—to rhyme beyond
Reason, as the French knew full well: bombast
As flowers of decadence abloom in Richmond.
    Poor Poe, to have died in someone else's clothes,
    Clothed now in a legend he would have loathed.

IN HER GARDEN
FOR TINA

In the sunlit glass reflection,
a figure glints
by the rosebush—pivot
for this moment and the next.

In the low green glade, adrift
among the trees by the stream,
a shimmer of light
and the sound of running water.

The scene embraces the unseen:
a breeze through a half-opened window,
a tangled braid of sound,
a feeling that rises with your name.

AT A FOUNTAIN IN ROME

What a lot of nothing it takes to make
something. Or, what a lot happens before
nothing happens—as when your work rises
out of emptiness to fill a blank, or
overflows as a fullness brimming,
the way a fountain's basin makes a curtain
of water, simultaneously
static and in continuous motion.
No one asks where the water comes from—
whether an ancient aqueduct carries it
or modern piping from some reservoir—
and no one cares where it goes, whether
circulating up or discharging into
storm drains and so on out to sea. It is
the present fall—the water glinting and
plashing in the morning air—that holds us,
lending freshness to our day. We are taken
up by that perpetual performance,
that cascade of illimitable water,
self-delighting and self-contained for all
its excess, as if an ecstatic body
were fixed in stone while an immanent grace
flowed out as everlasting as mortality
is for life—but life seen now from the other
side of life, a reflected image, where

past and future stretch on in panoramic
glory, but where the present moment is
blank, like the blind spot at the optic nerve,
a void not seen or noticed because folded
into the field of vision. Yet there it
remains, a sort of black hole from which no
time escapes but from which, were you to fall
into it, your life would issue again
in existence: flesh and blood, memory
and want, here, now, standing once more
before this flashing fountain, as it stands
in the light for what happens and what doesn't.

TWO-LINERS

PET THEORY

Those with dogs consider themselves cats;
those with cats know we're really dogs.

COLLATERAL DAMAGE

Every soldier is a civilian
to his weeping family.

FROM CRADLE TO GRAVE

Between the Tigris and the Euphrates:
the Alpha and Omega.

THE TOYMAKER'S CHILDREN

A sheet of paper, a stick of wood:
pleasure, the offspring of joy.

BUDDHIST MANQUÉ

Blind to worldly attachments:
out of mind, out of sight.

PRUDENCE AT THE DIRTY CAFÉ (1)

The man in the big white beard lights
his cigarette with his back to the wind.

HIGH-RISE TERMINAL

High-rise terminal: in linguistics,
"giving a statement the feel of a question."

Up at the High-rise Terminal
everything comes into question—
tickets, timetables, identities.
In the post-world nothing ends for certain,
each arrival a departure from the norm
until what's normal is the interrogative
interrogation that requests—or requires—
the phatic affirmative: the everlasting yea
downsized to a recessionary doubt
that words might coincide with sense.
"I see what you mean?" Yes, but what
is that hook at the end of everyone's phrase?
The information sign in the concourse
of concourse? At the High-rise Terminal
the Pyrrhonists have come into their own,
as every answer is another question.
"Hi, my name is Summer?" "Oh, really?"
But Socrates was right, the unexamined life
isn't worth living, so come on over
to the High-rise Terminal and see what's up?   69

MAVEN TO HER MIRROR

All beginnings are beyond their origins,
at once too late and premature.

I wasn't ready to leave
but ought to have months before.

The price we pay for premonitions
is regret—we know more than we know,

and less. "I saw it coming" means "I see it
going away." I stand in the middle,

Janus-faced, while events intersect me
at right angles. I see best obliquely.

If hindsight were foreknowledge
we would walk backwards,

like angels who fear to tread.
All my friends have separated—

the world is a centrifuge
and the results disorienting.

I thought love a circle but
it's an ellipse, with double foci,

mitosis the end result of marriage,
replication the new evolution.

In my solar system, planets
come and go like space shots.

I adjust for parallax
but satellites always fall to earth.

If I take a harsh tone
it's because I am distracted—

"I didn't mean it" means "I wasn't there."
When I die the funeral will be

the last time my friends come together.

UNCLE JOHN'S BAND

"We used to play for silver"

Even now our sound bears no name,
though we hang on the word of every song,
wondering what the night will bring
out of the flow and ebb and flow of time.

As if to know the earth's phase and feel
the orb skirt the day, we stand west,
facing a summer's sun burning at the edge
of tooled and gilded clouds, and to our eyes
sunset apprises the night's return.

A turn and shift of wind fills the air
with a sweeter, more moist and cooler taste.

Turning we behold behind us now, stretching
above the glowing hills of a further range,
storm clouds rising at a distance—twenty,
maybe fewer miles off—an echo of the sound.

Here, a moment—sudden in momentum—
a wind rushing along our bodies,
the music rearing to a whistling of the air—
another storm upon us.

Sweet remembrance, returning us to ourselves—
what stirs on the field below?
Thunder—gut-conceived, borne
by the song outright—claps "I am."

Rising to its final phase, the moon
breaks into waves washing the night—
blanched, rippling the ground gives way
to this our song bereft of words:

We are as nothing—we are all
filled with a violence our nature abhors.

"I am, I am" is all we ever sing.

TWO-LINERS

PECCADILLOES

With vices so refined, how could
his sins be but impeccable?

AGEIST

How is it that going downhill
is uphill all the way?

UNREAL ESTATE

The boom in the city sent
shock waves of greed to the country.

WHY SCHOOLS FAIL

Education is based on fear;
learning's beyond reproach.

PRUDENCE AT THE DIRTY CAFÉ (2)

The girl in the miniskirt and tank top considers
how best to retrieve her hairbrush on the floor.

TWO LADIES AND MAGRITTE AT THE MET

"This is not a pipe," explains Tina, translating.
"Why, then, what is it?" they ask.

V. ARGUMENT FROM DESIGN

ARGUMENT FROM DESIGN
ON THE TEA & COFFEE SET OF ILONKA KARASZ

Tell them, dear, that if eyes were made for seeing,
Then Beauty is its own excuse for being. EMERSON

Imagine a tea and coffee set
    (of cleanest, simplest design)
      on a silver-banded tray.
Imagine a family of four
    (father, mother, daughter, son)
      bound in a magic circle.

(I)

The ideal form is designed for use
    and when used up, the ideal remains.
    A pattern, a surface, explains
itself, being its own excuse.

No need here for the signature mark
    when every object has its aura—
    unique, undying, like Aurora
(not Tithonus, art's heresiarch).

Style is become a lexicon, yet
    art is craft when craft is art—"Design

79

Art" you call it, finer than Fine:
ideal *and* real (poet turns profit).

Take a line, a curve, spiral, circle...
    take the elements of form—motifs
    drawn on a well of beliefs—
and make the simple most masterful.

(II)

"You could not evade me, having spent all
those hours dusting and polishing the past.
I left my mark on you, as you on me—
this little dent, that careless scratch and scrape.
Did we ever take tea together? Or,
did I sit in the corner admired
until you came to me and held me close?
You see what shape I'm in now. We tarnish
with time, lines deepen, the substrate yellow.
But you recognized my picture right off
in that book? And here we are together.
Happy chance! (Though chance always feels fated.)
Why treat me with kid gloves—or cotton ones?
Take them off, touch me, feel my cool smoothness.
I was made to handle, though few could look
without emotion. I was special then,
and am officially so now. I've found

my place at last—though why the family
got rid of me I'll never understand.
Too much trouble, a little too classy?
At least they kept me together, else I'd
fall to pieces. You talk for a while now,
I want to hear your voice, hear it echo
within me. Yes? Our time is almost up.
Will you remember me to the others?
Tell them I'm every bit the same as when ...
Tell them I'm well here, surrounded by such
interesting types, some younger than I.
What? Am I reflected in your eyes?
Listen, we are all objects of desire."

(III)

Coffeepot

You stand over the others, your stature
undisputed, though the dark and even
bitter cup you offer cannot be given
to all guests. That's where the children's rapture

comes in, the one full of laughter and charm,
the other, lovely, pouring forth kindness.
Still, amelioration isn't blindness,
and the mother, also strong, means no harm

when she stands, not quite in opposition
(your aims are too similar for that) but
wholly as herself—seeking to disrupt
what she can't countenance or envision.

Always on your mettle, the blood can start
at the very sight of you, the pulse race
when seated before you face-to-face:
with designs upon us, you affect the heart.

Teapot

Ritual is design: that ceremony
each morning, a dish of tea, a biscuit,
the sun come to offer its testimony.
    Steeping, the teapot puts a lid on despair.

In a mural above the bed, St. Andrew
listens to the fish, as we watch to catch
a glimpse of how to understand you.
    Steeping, the teapot puts a lid on despair.

What moves below the flowing surface
remains mysterious. Depths are deceiving
and the bowl, aquamarine, thwarts our purpose.
    Steeping, the teapot puts a lid on despair.

Once, the mask slipped and the pain, apparent,
made a mirror of our gaze and shamed us.
Now we must acquire what we thought inherent.
    Weeping, the teapot put a lid on despair.

Creamer

Most open, most vulnerable—in a glance
you apprise of good fortune or mischance.

No one suffers quite like a daughter,
who, in unalloyed joy, is the author

of herself: the milk separate from the cream.
But this knowledge is dark—as though a dream.

To play your part you must know your place
and give everything over to efface

what you are: a silver vessel, not full,
not empty, but whole, graceful, never null.

Sugar Bowl

How you sweated that day in the heat!
Your shirt clung to your back in fear.

You shook with a fever that scared us.
What shook you would kill you next year.

Crystallized, hardened, you never lost
the sweetness that everyone loved.
A little of you went a long way.
When the push came, you knew to shove.

Your two sides showed in symmetry,
as if holding you took both hands.
You kept up appearances, kept your
distance: only withdrawal withstands.

Who could have borne all that promise
without thinking failure a crime?
You doled out grains from sugar cubes
as if hoarding the sands of time.

Tray

You house and embrace them,
the ideal image of the perfect
family—imperfections and all.

Who cares if the brass pins
holding you aren't original?
The home you came from,
an organic thing, with the defect

of its virtu, its blemished beauty, grew,
flowered, went to seed, to its origins.
It was built not to last, but to renew.
Like a tray, serving its purpose,
it held a family, and it moved us
to embrace and house you.

(IV)

Why did you select this piece?
    We were standing by the gravesite
    and the wind was in the spruce trees.

How well did you know the artist?
    A bell rang in the middle of the night
    and I climbed a flight of stairs.

Is this poem biographical?
    When we planted the garden
    the wild phlox stood round.

Why don't you answer these questions?
    Imagine a tea and coffee set
    bound in a magic circle.

AT KARACADAG

Steal this hour and put it in your pocket—
a talisman against the appointed hour

when tears well in the eyes of God
on the mountain of a Thousand and One Churches.

ALPHABET AT MORNING

Red bands cross the sky
in the half-light of early morning,
the woods fill with a raucous cry—
the a b c of every day.

Day now upon us,
already the need to resist the day,
turn the gain back to loss,
heed the night-work's warning.

Not to forget is hardest.
To be uncovered,
you recover the wish
to be simple as a, b, and c.

EUCHARIST AT MONT ST.-MICHEL

The novitiate hesitates for a moment
ascending the steps to the altar:

she is carrying the Offertory water and wine
to be transformed: sacrifice is on her mind,

the wheat and grapes of a life given
to redemption. She has been called but

does not know if she is chosen.
In the cloister garden outside, how long

has she agonized over it in early hours
and late, the chalice offered but not

yet drunk? As she hands the implements over,
the priest receives them with steady hands.

She bows and turns again to step down,
inscribing, over time, a whirling dance

to take her to the center of herself.
Once there, if nothing's discovered,

she will take the veil to die to this life.

FROM THE BOOK OF HOURS

He looks up from his book: out the window
the world is blue—as yesterday it was

red-orange beyond belief or disbelief—
steel-blue perhaps, but never mind, in this

moment it's blue to the unadjusted
eye. To see what he is seeing, that is

an illumination he seeks to paint.
His book will tell of how the hours fill us

as we would fill the hours, before our day
darkens to blue, red, and the darker night.

THE DESERT FATHER

Both virtues and vices make the mind blind:
with the first it does not see vices,
and with the second, virtues.

ABBA EVAGRIUS

Both virtues and vices make the mind blind—
so Abba Evagrius the Monk writes
from his solitary cell in Egypt.

Evagrius, son of a priest, had come
all the way from Constantinople in
flight from a "circumstance which threatened

his chastity"—better to take orders than
give free rein to free will in Byzantium,
city of glittering mosaic icons.

So the Abba, wide-eyed from warfare with
demons, attunes his soul to desireless
passion in the dry heat of the desert,

where at night cold stars cluster together,
mid-way between this world and all others
where virtues and vices blind the mind.

IN VIDA'S GARDEN

Brown and yellow leaves dapple
the lawn below four beech trees
in a sunken garden.

Branches above break the light
into patterns on the ground
and on the adobe wall.

Breezes short, swift and singing
subside as the sky's gold
medallion sun dazzles.

Brilliancy in such stillness
turns purposeful as we give
ourselves over to our work.

ENNEADS

He was unlike all others, other
than all those he made appear the same:
a blackened pine tree scarred by lightning,
singled out for a knowledge never
forgiven, struck by blazoned power
intolerable—the light whitening
around him, falling like a shower
on us, who first heard our secret name
and rose at its burden's lightening.

But then others came, and then more, such
that we despaired to know our true place—
there were so many with so little
to give, and they took much, far too much
for us or him to sustain, so down
that spiraling staircase of riddle
he went, speaking strangely and around
the central point, creating a space
all his own, all edge, with no middle.

We followed him to that edge and then
no further, for there was nowhere else
to go. We turned back only to find
he had turned his back on us, and when
most we needed him—or thought we did—

till suddenly there occurred a sign
for us that neither revealed nor hid
a truth, but showed what was false:
a disease of the eye—he'd gone blind.

How the blind see! Poet, prophet, man
of utter insight, the blinding stroke
turns the world inside out, draining shape
and color from form until the hand
reaches out to grasp the silhouettes
fading in the light, but they escape
in formlessness, the mocking objects
of our desire to believe. He spoke
of this, as of an inner landscape.

From then on, we knew our sole duty
was to open our eyes and for once
see as he saw us, unobscured by
form, sheer life visible, the beauty
of nothingness—and to find then form
as a coating that displays just why
we are opaque and cannot perform
the least service to ourselves: this blunts
self-regard—our life become our lie.

As you would expect, the death was hard
on us all, though surely least on him
who welcomed it as a sloughing off,

the body a skin of no regard,
though we buried it and mourned our loss—
but the voice we missed most, lilting soft,
then with harsh rebuke, as if to toss
aside some mask and unmake us limb
by limb, alien to ourselves, cast off

into shallows, where wallowing in
swamps of pity we picked ourselves up
in the end, purified by knowledge
of baseness. O, what a state to win
on this earth! But now who could debase
himself, walk out to the very ledge
and beyond? Before what god deface
the countenance of pride, how disrupt
the casual tide of sacrilege?

We had no answers, who only had
questions, and those unanswerable.
And the rhetoric of inquiry!
We could not stand our voices, the sad
mimicry and despair that laced
our words, until the iniquity—
the wheedling pretense—came to be faced.
Amidst decay, what was durable?
What could we wrest from our nullity?

And then we knew, we had understood
more than we knew, for in leaving us
he had left us ourselves, fraught with all
our diminishing flaws—yet we would
go on, like birds repopulating
a barren pond: seeds, parasites fall
as they breast the waters, negating
the emptiness around with surplus
of life. Do you grasp now why we call?

ON THE SABBATH
FOR KIEK ON HER BIRTHDAY

It was 10:30 in the morning, October 9th, 1994,
when Tina and I walked up the steps to your door

for a visit with you and Lutz, Maarten and his son.
It was a Sunday and as lovely an autumn day as one

could wish. We talked and ate and laughed and ate
some more, as you served us coffee and tea and cake.

We saw Lutz's shop below, your Work study room
above and then, after lunch, in the gold afternoon

we went for a long walk in a wooded park
with oak trees and flowers and, in the dark

shadows, mushrooms growing with a fragrance
Lutz paused to smell. All the abundance

of life was with us then—as it is now
and is meant to be, for memory is how

we remember ourselves and Work is the path
we are walking still, when every day is the Sabbath.

TOBIAS AND THE ANGEL

And Raphael was sent to heal them both,
that is, to scale away the whiteness of Tobit's
eyes, and to give Sara the daughter of Raguel
for a wife to Tobias the son of Tobit; and to
bind Asmodeus the evil spirit. TOBIT 3:17

Was it enough to walk with him
beyond the dry hills of Nineveh,
enough to roast fish together
on the banks of the Tigris?

I knew him as a countryman but
not for what he was, unknowable,
a voice in the stricken night, crying
"I am brethren, I will bind you to me."

Such a distance to travel, under
a milky sky, with dust in the air, sharp
pebbles underfoot, birds raucous in trees,
and the puzzlement of his eyes.

What more could I take in but that
tone, that surety hanging like a cloud
about him? Even my dog staggered
in his presence. What question could I frame?

97

Blindness he could cure, yet one day
half-blind himself he and I carried a table
through a doorway and up the long
passage, as if we both might thereby see.

Later, a vision of my father, of gall
anointing his upturned face, of whiteness
pilling away from the corners of his eyes
and he falling upon my neck and weeping.

I had no such tears to offer, knowing
so little what time brings, the sacred
affliction, the unsought recompense
on the outskirts of the waking town.

And what of Sara and the dark angel?
I was mad to wed her, trembling
on the threshold—whether desiring her flesh
or my death, I could not distinguish.

In twos and threes and then decades
at a time, the years passed as I prospered.
Was it enough to attend to his words
now that words are no longer enough?

ON EARTH

How did you spend your time?

In spring, I heard birds
sing out in voices
larger than themselves.

And then how did you spend your time?

In the evenings in summer
fireflies brought stars
down from the sky.

How did you spend your time?

In autumn a maple tree
swayed in the wind, its branches
flickering an orange fire.

Then how did you spend your time?

In winter, I watched
snow put the land to sleep—
then woke to your voice.

99

ACKNOWLEDGEMENTS

The following poems originally appeared elsewhere in journals and anthologies: "Doo Town," "A Whiter Shade of Pale," *Australian Book Review*; "A Myth of Justice," *Guernica*; "A Portent," *Kenyon Review*; "Tobias and the Angel," "The Desert Father," "Enneads," *Notre Dame Review*; "Two Trees," "Like Life Itself," *Paris Review*; "No Photo. Go Home," "To Make a Desert," *PEN America*; "For My Father Dying," *Space*; "Knowing," "Admiralty Bay," "The Koan," *Verse*; "Argument from Design," *Words for Images: A Gallery of Poems*; "Third Parent," *Vintage*; "Teen Town," *Best Australian Poems 2004*.

"Psyche" was first published in a limited edition as a Warwick Publications Chapbook, 2006.

Grateful acknowledgement is made to The Susan Turner Fund at Vassar College for assistance with this book and to Mary Jo Salter for her detailed comments on the manuscript.

ABOUT THE AUTHOR

Paul Kane is the author of two previous collections of poems, *The Farther Shore* and *Drowned Lands*. His other publications include a critical study of Australian poetry, an edition of Ralph Waldo Emerson's poems, a collaboration with the photographer William Clift, and several anthologies. A recipient of fellowships from the National Endowment for the Humanities and the Guggenheim Foundation, he has also been awarded Fulbright and Mellon grants. He teaches at Vassar College and lives in Warwick, New York.

Printed in the USA
CPSIA information can be obtained
at www.ICGtesting.com
JSHW080002150824
68134JS00021B/2223